WHEN THE HECK
DID THAT HAPPEN?

A WOMAN'S GUIDE TO TURNING 50 AND BEYOND

KAREN SAXE EPPLEY

Muse Media
2275 Dandridge Drive
York PA 17403
karen@whentheheck.com

ISBN: 979-8-89704-574-7 (Paperback)
ISBN: 979-8-89704-573-0 (ebook)

DISCLAIMER

This work is for entertainment purposes only. The advice and strategies contained herein may not be suitable for every situation. This work is sold with the understanding that the Publisher is not engaged in rendering medical, legal, accounting or other professional services. If professional assistance is required, the services of a competent professional person should be sought.

To my mom, Rachel,
a beautiful role model who taught
me to be strong and age gracefully.

To my daughter, Ada,
my greatest Earthly treasure.
May I continue to raise you to be a strong,
independent, and fearless woman today and
well past your 50s.

ACKNOWLEDGEMENTS

No book is just one person's effort. I have had so much inspiration and support in the creation of *When The Heck Did That Happen*.

A big thank you to...

The ladies who shared their stories to show us how it should (or should not) be done.

The authors who have taught me about publishing and promotion – Vickie Helm and Dave Romeo.

My editors, Steve Eppley, Kim Romeo, and Dave Romeo for their invaluable input.

To my husband, Steve, who has encouraged me through all my crazy adventures, including this book.

AND YOU for purchasing this book and encouraging me with your positive feedback.

TABLE OF CONTENTS

PROLOGUE

Do you remember it? The first time some-one called you, *"Ma'am?"* I can't tell you exactly when or where it was, but I vividly remember the feeling. I was stunned. I think the world actually stopped spinning on its axis for a moment.

"I am a Miss, not a Ma'am," my mind screamed. *"I am too young to be a Ma'am."*

That moment was indicative of the roller coaster ride called Womanhood.

Buckle up, Ladies. It's a bumpy ride!

WHERE IT STARTED

I always wanted to write a book. I started one once. It was 365 of my favorite motivational and funny quotes. But my motivation drifted away and it's still in my computer somewhere. Then, a new book began to whirl around in my almost 50-year-old mind.

When I was approaching 50, I had perceptions of the good, the bad, and the ugly about "The Big 5-0." Most of my excitement was the rumor that at 50 your filters begin to evaporate and you become less concerned about what people think of you. As a lifelong perfectionist and people-pleaser, I relished walking through that magic curtain. And sure enough, I turned 50 and the filters began to disappear!

I also heard whisperings about the physical changes that awaited me. And, by golly, at age 50 years and one day, it started to happen. My knees began to creak, getting out of a chair was a bit of a challenge, and I won't even tell you about what I saw in the mirror that morning! At that moment, I blurted out the title of this book... *"When the heck did that happen?!"* I realized I needed a survival guide to maneuver through this new chapter of my life. I bet you do too.

It took until I was 63, when my 50th birthday was in the rearview mirror, to dust off my notes and begin to write. I successfully survived my 50s. Now is the time to share my joys, bruises (physically and mentally), and funny adventures with you.

While researching this book I found a college paper I wrote in the 1980s. As I look back on *"Midlife for the American Female: Crisis or Not,"* I see how far we have come and how far the American culture has to go. (By the way, I got an A.)

I had a lot of help and inspiration while writing this book. My dear friend, Jennifer, is exactly five months and two days older than me. I have to confess that I do relish that she is older. I have watched her graduate into each new year with wisdom and beauty. She is an inspiration. (I did mention that she is older than I am, right? Silly me, I do love to say that.)

Dozens of other women shared their stories with me. In this book, I state each story as my own to *"protect the bashful"* from their embarrassing experiences. Hey, we are on this journey together!

Ultimately, that is the point of this book. It isn't just you. The over-50 journey crosses every race, religion, and socioeconomic class. Every woman experiences the joys and challenges of these life changes. We need to stand by each other, support each other, and laugh with each other as we survive this thing called life. No matter your age, always remember...

You are strong.
You are smart.
You are brave.
You are beautiful.

CHAPTER 1

WHEN THE HECK DID THAT HAPPEN?

It may appear stereotypical to begin a book for women with a chapter on appearance. But we experience most of the initial changes of aging in our bodies. My face was the first site of many *"when the heck"* moments.

The Eyes Have It

I've always smiled a lot. I deflected many compliments about my smile by saying, *"I might as well give these smile lines a reason to be there."* Then came that day I realized my *"smile lines"* were there even when I wasn't smiling.

Pride is another reason for *"smile lines."* Most of us don't begin wearing glasses until after we have been squinting for a while.

At some point, we all will probably need reading glasses. You know, the things you can't find when you need them? (FYI: check the top of your head first.)

Your search for your reading glasses often begins at inopportune times: when you just sit down or get into bed, when you sit on the toilet with a good book, and when you put on your makeup. Here are a few tips I (eventually) learned that might help you:

1. Even if you have invested in a *"good pair"* of readers from your eye doctor, buy readers from the drug store or dollar store... a lot of them. Make sure you have a pair in key places: bedroom, bathroom, office, reading chair... wherever you might need them.

2. I put my readers in the same color eyeglass cases in each location to avoid confusing them with my husband's or having him pick up mine. It also disciplines me to put them away so I know where they are when I need them.

3. Put a drop of bright nail polish on the top of all of your clear lids and caps for skin-care and makeup. I used to regularly lose the clear caps on my bathroom counter when I was doing my skincare routine. Even without glasses, I can still see those bright colors.

It is time to give up your eyeglasses-pride. I am past the *"I don't look good in glasses"* vanity. I am more concerned with actually seeing. I have also accepted giving up the smell and feel of cracking open a new book. (Except this one, of course.)

My husband has been reading books on his tablet for years. I always thought it was sacrilege and touted that I would never use a Kindle. Fast forward a couple of years. I now enjoy all my books on Kindle. I love having dozens of books loaded onto my tablet. The ability to increase the font size is good too.

By the way, this book is printed in 14 pt type to help both of us read a little easier.

But Wait, There's More!

Don't worry about those pesky little wrinkles because there is more to come. Age spots, rosacea, and marionette lines. Oh my!

The good (or bad) news is that it often comes down to genes. From any age, you can get an indication of how you are going to look in a few years by staring at your mom and grandma. (Don't stare too long because it really freaks them out.) Your genes can determine the amount of collagen your body produces, your bone structure, and other fun body facts that we'll discuss in Chapter 3.

There are a few factors that you *can't* applaud or blame on your genes. How do you take care of your skin? I won't go into the dangers to your lungs and overall health from smoking. But if those reasons don't make you quit, think of your face. Smoking ages your skin and especially your face. BIG time. If you want your face to look like an elephant's backside, keep smoking. If not, throw the cigs away!

Smoking isn't the only thing that can make your skin look like age-spotted leather. Too much sun can do damage too. I am not a swimmer, but I was a pool bunny – you know, the woman who lies by the pool to catch some rays in a tiny bikini that should never get wet because it might shrink even more. I didn't just lie in the sun, I coated myself in baby oil to get more sun. Yep, I graduated Cum Laude from the same college whose courtyard I baked in baby oil. Brilliant.

And Still More...

There are a few more gifts that come with aging... keratoses, varicose veins, and that hangy-down skin under your arms.

Clothing can hide a lot of our body changes. At least for a while.

But our faces are out there every day for the world to see. As we age, reduced collagen and environmental conditions may cause wrinkles, skin that looks dull and not as lush and moist as in the past, and the circles under our eyes may darken. (Feeling good about yourself yet?)

There are a multitude of creams, serums, and promises from cosmetic companies. But the best way to keep our skin looking as healthy and youthful as possible is simple.

At minimum:

1. Wash your face with a gentle cleanser EVERY morning and night. Wash away environmental toxins, facial oil, and dirt to cleanse pores for healthier-looking skin.

2. Drink a lot of water. Water is our life... literally. Multiple internet sites (because we know the internet is never wrong) state that women's bodies are 55-60% water. One can die from dehydration before starvation or sleep deprivation.

3. Stop smoking and limit sun exposure. In addition to all the other damage smoking and too much sun can present, both age your skin greatly. All those *"cool"* cigarettes and sun-kissed tans may not look so cool or kissable in the future.

Ears And Noses

Remember the show, *"Two and a Half Men?"* Charlie Harper was a womanizing man who only engaged in extracurricular activities with younger women. When someone tried to set him up with a woman his own age, Charlie was not pleased. In his tirade, he mentioned that women's ears and noses continue to grow as they get older. His final statement was something like, "I bet she's got some ears on her. A good wind and she'll probably fly away."

Unfortunately for women (and men), two things we usually can't change are our ears and nose. Yep, on top of everything else, we run the risk of looking like a Dumbo/Pinocchio hybrid. The fun never ends.

Speaking Of Celebrities

I learned a very important lesson when I turned 60. Actresses and other *"beautiful people"* aren't perfect. Who knew?

I was watching TV and realized Jennifer Aniston, Iman, and Oprah don't have perfect faces. Just like us, their eyes are different sizes, their faces aren't symmetrical, and... wait for it... they have wrinkles! They are human, just like us!

WARNING: After you realize this, you will never be able to see a beautiful woman without realizing that their face is not perfect. You will see that you are as, or more, stunning than they are.

Furrows, They Aren't Just For Farmers Anymore

Have you ever heard the phrase, *"a furrowed brow?"* That is because the weight of the world that sits on your shoulders is also sitting on your forehead.

The furrows on my brow were pretty deep. I say *"were"* because I succumbed to my vanity and got Botox. I am NOT recommending Botox or any other face enhancement to you or anyone else. For decades, I said, *"I will never allow the pressures of our media, culture, or a man to force me to hide my age with a facelift."* I don't plan on getting a facelift, but I did choose Botox for me.

I wasn't bothered by my age, but my furrowed brow really bothered me. I wasn't trying to look perfect, hide who I was, or look like Joan Rivers. I wanted to look more like me again. I've done it more than once. I don't regret it.

But don't tell anyone. I want them to think it's natural. Yeah, sure. But it makes me happy and that's all that counts.

A Few More Things

There are a few tips that have been shared with me over time that have helped me (and my face) feel happier:

1. Sleep on your back. Your pillow is a problem. That big lumpy thing under your head each night that you keep saying you are going to replace, is messing with your face. It is pulling your skin when you lie on your side. Pulling the thinner skin on your face creates creases and wrinkles. Don't do

that. One negative thing about sleeping on your back is that you will probably generate more work for yourself when you notice the cobwebs on the walls and ceiling fan. By the way, it's time to paint your ceiling.

2. If you don't have a skin care routine, it is time to start. The most important thing is a clean face at least once a day, but preferably morning and night. And do not use soap! It dries the skin on your face which is different from the other skin on your body.

3. Invest in skincare products, especially a cleanser and moisturizer with sunscreen. You don't have to spend a fortune. Drugstore brands are perfectly fine. Just find the one that works best for your skin. If you do choose to spend more on your skincare, I recommend medical-grade products from a cosmetic dermatologist or med spa.

4. Don't forget your neck. I have seen many women with impeccable skin on their face because they take care of it. Then I look down a little farther and I see their grandma's neck. Unless you intend to wear tur-

tlenecks every day and night, whatever you do to your face, do to your neck.

And then there is makeup:

1. Don't try to hide behind more makeup. Too much makeup didn't look good when you were 20. It doesn't look good now.

2. Buy the right makeup. Our skin isn't the same as it was in our 20s and 30s. Our makeup shouldn't be either. The wrong makeup cakes in our small wrinkles and large pores. Not pretty.

3. Do not try to wear the latest fad for 20-somethings. It doesn't work for us. An example is the currently popular *"cat eyes."* The eye liner that extends past the corner of your eye usually gets caught in a laugh line, then you have to lift your eyelid to end the line. Not sexy.

4. Do not *heavily* draw your eyebrows with an eyebrow pencil. It does not look natural. Fortunately, there are a lot of new products that look more natural. But please don't

look like my Aunt Trudy with her heavily penciled brows that come up to a point in the middle. It looks... well, it just looks.

Final Thoughts

I have a tag from a Mary Kay product taped inside my closet door. It says *"BeYOUtiful YOU."* We all need that reminder sometimes. If you need a reminder, tape a special message inside your closet door... or go watch TV and see all the beautiful, not perfect, people.

"The most beautiful thing you can wear is confidence."
– Blake Lively

CHAPTER 2

THE HAIR DOWN THERE AND OTHER SCARY STORIES

There's no getting around it. When you find that first white pubic hair, your first reaction is usually disbelief followed by a resounding, *"AH-HHH!"*

While we don't necessarily feel good about the first gray hair in our eyebrow or on the top of our head, this is different. This is *"down there."* Our most private place. But it is worse than that. Most pubic hair doesn't turn gray. It turns white!

And now the *"little white hair fairy"* has slipped into our panties and waved her magic wand.

Don't worry. You are not alone in this moment of distress. Based on a statistically stratified random sample... Well, ok, it was three girlfriends, a Friday night, and a bottle of wine, but nonetheless... that FIRST white pubic hair is the most traumatic.

I don't choose to dye my pubic hair, but there is a market for it. In 2008, betty™ introduced *Color For The Hair Down There*. The company offers traditional black, brown, and blonde for those looking for a perfect match. For the more adventurous consumer, betty™ also sells hot pink, bright blue, red, and purple. If you are interested in coloring the white hair in your panties, or just going a little wild, check out bettybeauty.com. I won't tell.

Coloring Your Up-There Hair

Dyeing the hair on top of your head is common. Adding highlights, becoming the color you always wanted, or having fun with bright greens, purples, or reds don many a head.

During college, I began coloring my hair, not to cover gray but for fun to change my God-given mousey brown. I still enjoy the shine of the color I wish I had been born with but I must confess, I happily cover my gray now.

In this culture where hair dye covers the tresses of many women (and men), it is important to remember three key tips before you color:

1. Invest in good hair color. Whether you have it done at a salon or you color at home, research products then choose wisely. A poor quality hair dye can damage your hair. I love Madison Reed™ at madison-reed.com.

2. Choose the right color for you. Just because you used a specific color when you were younger, doesn't mean it is the right color now. In most cases a lighter shade is best. It covers the gray more naturally and probably works better with your changing skin tone. Remember, you don't want to look like the guy who shows up to work one day looking like he dyed his hair with black shoe polish.

3. I love the bold pink, purple, blue, and green dyes out there today. But for the love of chocolate, do not put *blue rinse* on your gray hair like my grandmas did! What was

that stylist thinking when he turned beautiful white-haired ladies into Smurfs?

I respect women who choose not to color their hair. Go gray naturally. With the right haircut, it can be striking. But I would not choose the option of a cashier I saw at a store right after COVID. She was the poster child for *"how not to do it."* Her gray/white hair hung straight to her shoulders, then the rest of her hip-length hair was dark brown. Do not do this at home... or any place else for that matter.

It's Where?

Something about getting older is that hair tries to escape out of your body any place it wants: necks, chins, upper lips, ears, noses, and other places. And to make it worse, those sneaky hairs are usually hard and stick out. It might as well have a flashing neon light on it!

The first stray hair that snuck up on me was in my 20s. I saw a single hair sticking out of my neck. I couldn't grab it with my fingers, so I grabbed a pair of tweezers and pulled and pulled and pulled. A two-inch hair came out of my neck! I was totally freaked out. Was this going to be a regular thing for me? Oh no!

I am happy to report I never extracted another long hair out of my body. But then there is my nose. I have seen bushy nose hair on men, never women. I never saw bushy nose hair coming out of me. But during a regular hair appointment, my stylist got a good view up my nostrils when he washed my hair. He blurted out, *"It's time."* Huh? He told me that my nose hairs were sprouting like the Amazon rainforest. They hadn't reached the end of my nostrils yet but they would be. What? My nose hairs were going to look like my Uncle Louie's! I rushed to the local drug store to buy a nose hair trimmer – which I had to get in the men's section. Apparently not a single woman in the universe, except me, has aggressive nose hairs.

I have since learned that there are more women like me. As a matter of fact, nose hair trimmers can be found in the women's section in lovely shades of pink, purple, and fluorescent green because that is definitely a bathroom accessory to which we want to draw attention. It will also remind us that Einstein's crazy hair will be exiting our noses any day now.

When Thin Isn't So Great

Like men, some women's hair thins or doesn't grow as quickly as they age. If you choose, there are products to help thicken the hair you have and help it grow a bit faster. There are hair extensions, and even hair pieces. But do not feel like you have to *"fix it."* Embrace the change. Do crazy things with hats and headbands. You are beautiful just the way you are! It is your choice to believe that. It is your choice to do anything you want with your hair. *Except a blue rinse. Please do not do a blue rinse.*

And speaking of pubic hair – yes, we are talking about that again. Let me tell you an embarrassing story. Several years ago, I decided to do what *"every woman"* was doing. (That should have been my first hint at disaster.) Ladies were waxing and shaving their pubic hair to a Brazilian (no hair), Runway (thin strip down the middle), or various designs (I understand hearts are popular.) Bottom line (or should I say front line) is that I did it. First, it was weird, not appreciated by my partner and was uncomfortable when it started to grow out. But, there is more. As a 50+ woman, my hair is growing a lot slower than it used to. Like years! My hair down there definitely doesn't look the same.

In the future, maybe I should avoid what *"everyone"* is doing.

There Are Advantages

There is a wonderful benefit from thin, slow-growing hair. You don't have to shave your legs very often! Any excuse not to bleed from careless shaving is good for me.

"Invest in your hair. It is the crown
you never take off."
– Unknown

CHAPTER 3

BODIES, BOOBIES, AND BEAUTY

For many people, a photograph is their downfall. For me, it was a photo at my friend Lynn's wedding. As I went through the photos, I saw a chubby chick that looked a lot like me. I knew I had picked up a few pounds, but WOW! People told me, *"the camera adds a few pounds."* There must have been several cameras taking that photo because it showed I had gained a lot more than the previously suspected "few pounds."

I took the only obvious action. I put down the bowl of ice cream I was eating to make a note to myself to tell anyone who attempted to take my photo that I am an Amish Vampire in the Witness Protection Program. That should keep them away.

Out Of The Mouths Of Babes

We adopted our daughter when she was 22 months old; I was 48. I love being an older mom. But occasionally I am reminded that I am the age of her friends' grandparents.

When my daughter was about six, we were showering in the locker room after a swim. She was talking to me, then suddenly stopped. She was staring at my breasts with fascination. She pointed at my chest and asked, *"Didn't your boobies used to be up there?"* After we had a good laugh, it occurred to me that in just a short six years my body had changed enough for my little girl to notice. I already knew my body was changing. Gravity was becoming less and less of my friend. What I didn't realize is that other people noticed.

Let's face it. I don't look like I did when I was 20 or 30 or 40. And since I am 63, I don't look like I did when I was 50, either.

Most of us are not a size four; nor do we have incredible never-grow-older genes. Most of us don't have the time to prepare special diets or workout daily. We gotta work with what we've got.

Our Culture Can Be Cruel

My mom is a beautiful woman. I have a school picture of her when she was 14. She looks like a young Jackie Onassis. Yep, drop dead gorgeous. I am sure the boys in her high school drooled.

But when my 30-something-year-young mom was walking through my high school halls with me, a group of eager, high school boys were behind us talking about *"the new student"* and how hot she was. Mom stood a little taller, until one of the boys said, *"Eww guys. Look at her face. She's old."* Granted he was a pimply-faced, testosterone-racing, cheerleader-chasing high school boy but, that is when it starts.

On a side note, it is really gross (high school word) when guys of any age hit on your mom in front of you.

Our culture can be hard on women because of their appearance. Social media is full of body shaming. There are thousands of products that tell us how we should look. Models have tiny waists and bums, and TV has 20-year-olds selling wrinkle cream.

But always remember and never forget, beauty is the way YOU define it, and beauty looks just like YOU!

Grandma's Girl

In my 30s, I was sitting on a ridiculously low sofa. As I pulled myself out, I made a grandma sound. Well, at least my grandma. The sound that escaped my lips was a low groan, followed by *"Oh baby."* My almost 70-year-old grandma made that sound every time she stood up!

A moan and *"Oh baby"* became a regular phrase in my vocabulary, and not in a good way. Why did it have to be *"Oh baby?"* Why not *"How 'bout them Yankees"* or *"Let's go get a pizza?"*

As I got older, I inherited a few more of grandma's traits. My hands, calves, and feet are identical twins with hers. Unfortunately, they were not her greatest assets.

Dove Gets It

I appreciate the major retailers who embrace the truth that healthy, happy women come in all shapes and sizes. For example, the Dove Corporation developed a *Real Beauty Pledge*. Without apologies, Dove features real women in its advertising. Different sizes, shapes, ethnicities, hair color, and styles. No models. No retouching.

I love one of the statements in Dove's Pledge... *"We never present the unachievable, manipulated, flawless images of 'perfect' beauty which the use of retouching tools can promote."* Thank you, Dove.

Now Is The Time For Us To "Get It"

In March 2019, an annual Women's National Health Awareness event reported 80 percent of women in the U.S. are dissatisfied with their appearance. We (yes, me too) need to stop being one of those women!

Let's take a step back. Do you remember the time in your life when you had the body you would love to have had your whole life? Whether that was curvy and voluptuous, or lean and slender, it is the body that makes you think, *"I would like to have that body again."*

As children, and maybe into our early adulthood, most of us were super lean or just plain skinny. As womanhood kicked in, the curves began and so did other changes. Our hips got a little wider while our flat bellies became a little rounder.

I was a late bloomer. My changes happened in my late 20s. The good news was that I finally grew breasts! I no longer have the chest of a pre-pubescent boy!

But there were other changes. I remember sitting in the bathtub staring at my small round belly. Surely, I had to be pregnant for this *"huge"* round thing to appear overnight. Fortunately, it was just a big dinner and not enough exercise to keep my stomach muscles firm. But still.

If you are one of the disciplined women who eat smart and exercise faithfully to keep your body the way you want it, God bless you. If you are one of the women who are genetically blessed with the body you want, I am happy for you.

But please understand that some of us are envious of you. Please be gentle with us.

But Here Is The Most Important Beauty Tip

In my 20s, many people called me "beautiful." I modeled in fashion shows. A local department store asked me to model in its next circular. The pictures were taken by the premier photographer in Baltimore. The other models' photos were spectacular. Mine were awful!

That is when I learned the truth about beauty. I was not as physically beautiful as people thought I was. It was my beautiful spirit and approach to life that showed through. THAT is what made me attractive. A two-dimensional photo can't show that. Beauty at every age is what people really see inside of us.

A Real Beauty

At 91, Carmen Dell'Orefice is the world's oldest working supermodel. Carmen was a cover model for Vogue when she was 15. This silver-haired beauty is still strutting down runways.

In 2022, Carmen did a nude photoshoot for a cover story in *New You* magazine... yep, buck naked. Draped in a white silk sheet in a luxurious white bedroom, Carmen rocked it!

Carmen has something that many of us don't have... inner confidence, pride in who she is, and a willingness to put herself out there.

The Bottom Line...

You are beautiful! Own it.

Every morning since my daughter was four, I have told her, *"You are strong. You are smart.*

You are brave. You are beautiful." When she is nervous or scared, we repeat that affirmation together. Affirmations are powerful. They remind your mind of the truth.

You are beautiful! Embrace it.

Stop listening to the toxic stories your mind is telling you. When you accept them, you may start seeking validation from other people and outside sources. They don't know you. Don't let others give you their toxic messages.

You are beautiful! Accept it.

*"Kindness makes you beautiful and
looks better on you than
any clothes you wear."*
– Unknown

CHAPTER 4

MAMMOGRAMS, MENOPAUSE, AND OTHER CRUEL TRICKS OF NATURE

Doctors are always part of our lives, but as we get older we usually visit more often. And, oh what fun it is.

Many doctors failed to take (or just failed) their *"proper communication with patients"* class. Hence, at some point you may hear, *"for a woman your age..."* Since smacking your doc is against the law, I have no recommendations for you.

But my gynecologist took *"for a woman your age"* to a whole new level. During that fun time when your feet are in stirrups, my doctor looked inside 50-year-old me, looked at my folder, then looked inside again. His head peered up between my knees and said, *"Your face looks like you're 30 (nice compliment), but your vagina looks like an 80-year-old.*" I didn't know what to say to that. He definitely failed the patient communication class!

Ouch

You have probably been getting mammograms every year since your 20s. They weren't fun then and they aren't fun now. (A man invented it... for real, Raul Leborgne in 1949.)

Because my family doesn't have a history of breast cancer, I am happy to report that since I turned 60, I only need to get a mammogram every five years! I hope you are equally blessed.

You Gotta Love Menopause

Whether you are perimenopausal, postmenopausal or in the throes of hot flashes, night sweats, and mood swings, I have bad news. Your body is changing... again.

The average American woman gains 10-15 pounds during perimenopause and menopause. The weight gain is generally in the belly. Great.

But wait, there's more. Our metabolism makes it harder to lose weight. This is where men usually lose weight faster than women. It surprises me that there aren't more male homicides during this time of our lives.

Menopausal stress and discomfort often produce stress eating. We can follow the many medical recommendations of more fiber and protein, more sleep, 200 less calories, and 60 minutes of exercise a day. Yeah, right. Bring on the ice cream, cookies, and Milky Ways!

"Nothing makes a woman more beautiful than the belief that she is beautiful."
– Sophia Loren

CHAPTER 5

PEOPLE SAY STUPID THINGS

I've said them. You've said them. People are never at a loss for saying stupid things.

Like the time I asked the woman in the elevator when she was due... twice. Yeah, you guessed it. She wasn't pregnant either time.

Young'uns

Sometimes younger people unintentionally say things to people older than them. The list is endless, but here is an example that happened to me.

I needed a quick picture of myself. Picture (pun intended) a 22-year-old non-professional photographer taking an unplanned photo of a 50-year-old me. It wasn't pretty... the situation or the photo. Shawn kept saying, *"There is some-*

thing wrong with your neck. Can you fix it?" In my head I said, *"No, young'un. I am getting older. My neck is crepey. I would fix it if I could."* My voice said, *"Just work with it."*

When 20 Was Old

When we were very young, we used to think 20 was old and 30 was ready for the grave. That number changed to 50, then 100. I love the advertising *"50 is the new 40."* Sounds like a bunch of young marketing people sucking up to sell something to us.

Chronological age means little to me. I truly believe age is a frame of mind. Today, I am chronologically 63. But some days I'm 30... other days I'm 80.

People younger than us say inappropriate things, but then so did we when we were younger.

1. Did they have electricity when you were little?

2. Did you know they used to have phones that plugged into the wall?

3. Do you listen to JayZ? Oh, wait. You are old, probably not.

I even had an intern candidate who came into my office and said, *"I knew you were old. You use punctuation in your texts."* (She did not get the job.)

Speaking Of Speaking Differently

Many people in the younger generations seem to prefer to communicate via text instead of phone calls. Their communication includes abbreviations like LOL (laugh out loud.) We can use this shorthand too, but it is important to stay current.

When I was growing up, LOL meant (lots of love.) A 70-year-old neighbor started texting and wanted to use *"the lingo."* He began adding LOL (lots of love, he thought) to many of his texts. Sorry to hear of your husband's passing LOL (Laugh Out Loud.) Get well soon LOL (Laugh Out Loud.) Oops.

When young people do speak, their texting shortcuts infiltrate their spoken words. I was talking with my then 14-year-old and she told me a funny story. She ended her story with *"LOL, happy emoji."* Huh?

There are other short-speaks created by the younger generation. *"Do you want to come with?"* With what? Is it so hard to add *"me?"*

Where's The Beef?

As a professional marketer, I understand creating a message for your target audience. For example, I would never create a commercial for an antidiarrheal targeting young people with grandpa running to the bathroom.

Have you ever seen an ad or commercial when afterward you said, *"I don't understand it."* I used to tell my husband (who is 10 years older than me), *"Honey, those commercials aren't targeted to you so they aren't designed to speak to you."* Today, I don't get most of them either. Enough said.

A Time And Place

Younger people are a valuable resource when you get a new computer, TV remote, or even microwave. They grew up with technology. It is second nature to them. Me? Not so much.

When I was growing up, TV remotes were connected by a cord. My first computer was at work in my late teens. Remember the big beige boxes with green text on black screens?

Even preschoolers can master technology better than I can at times. My then three-year-old daughter figured out pay-per-view before I did. I found this out when I walked into the living room to find her watching pay-per-view porn. Yes, it was another *"proud parenting moment."* Ugh.

Stupid Things Are Not Just From Younger People

Recently I heard a man say, *"I feel bad for actresses. They have a short window of time when they are young and beautiful, then nobody wants them again until they can play old grandmothers."* Hmm. Let me get this straight.

1. We are no longer beautiful after our 20s and 30s?

2. Most of our peers are grandmothers, so we are old?

I held my tongue for fear I would go ballistic. Grrrrrr!

Sometimes It Is You

One of the benefits of the Big 5-0 and beyond is that some of our filters dissolve without us being aware of it. For me, I suddenly felt like I didn't have to be a people-pleaser or something I wasn't. And I liked it! As long as I am not hurting anyone, I am more inclined to say what I think instead of when I was 49 and younger. Life is good!

For example:

1. It is OK if you don't like me. I may have cared when I was 30, but I don't anymore.

2. No, I can't help you today.

3. Yes, I am eating ice cream for breakfast.

"Age is an issue of mind over matter.
If you don't mind, it doesn't matter."
– Mark Twain

CHAPTER 6

(DON'T) ACT YOUR AGE

Remember when you were younger and adults used to tell you to *"act your age"*? Well, this is the time to define for yourself what *"acting your age"* looks like. Your definition of being 50+ will probably be different from your mom's and grandma's. It can also look differently from the 50-year-old next door. You get to decide.

Yes, you can! You can climb Mount McKinley. You can go skydiving. You can learn how to sail. You can sit outside and read all day. You can go skinny dipping. The list is endless. It is based on your abilities, interests, and passions.

In February 2023, 98-year-old Betty Linberg ran a 5K. After shattering the world record in 2022, Betty Lindberg ran the Publix Atlanta 5K in a blazing 59 minutes, and 6 seconds. Betty is not old because she doesn't think she is. Betty refuses to *"act her age."*

We Are Older, Not Old

We should never deny our age. Embrace it. Yes, we are older than we used to be, but we are not old! Consider this, at this very moment you are younger than you will ever be again. Whether you are talking about moments or decades, your age doesn't matter. You get to choose what it means to *"act your age."*

My dad visited a 106-year-old family friend in a nursing home. He asked her if there were any good-looking men there for her. She answered, *"No, they are all old."* You gotta love a lady with standards.

Yes, You Can

Don't fall into the *"I couldn't possibly"* trap. Since she was a little girl, I taught my daughter that *"can't"* is a bad word. Now I am going to teach you.

You can... within your physical, mental, emotional, psychological, financial, and spiritual abilities. You want to run a marathon. OK, you may not be in the physical shape to run it today, but you can train (like every other marathon runner.)

If you want it, don't let your age be your excuse not to do it. If you have other reasons, that is fine. But never let your reason be your age.

Yes, You Can Get Out

Multiple scientific and psychological studies show that isolation, particularly in older adults, has negative effects on physical and mental health, and longevity. Whether you meet a friend for coffee, go to a rumba class, or something in between, get out of the house. It may just be going grocery shopping to be around people. As Nike says... *Just Do It*. As I say... *Just Do Something*.

As you age, you may feel tired or think you just want to stay in (again.) Inactivity breeds inactivity. Don't get caught in that rut. Don't want to drive at night? No problem. Go out with a friend and ask her to drive. There is also Uber and paratransit. No excuses.

Respect A Few Important Rules

1. Don't hang out with old people. Old has little to do with chronological age and more with mindset. Jim Rohn said, *"You are the average of the five people you spend the most time with."* Don't let other people make you *"old."*

2. Don't wear tube tops or anything else that you think will make you look like your granddaughter. If you are the one in a bazillion 50+ age women who can rock a tube top, do it if you want. But the rest of us should never, I repeat NEVER, wear tube tops. With that said, don't relegate your wardrobe to granny panties and mom jeans. Wear what you like that *looks good on you.*

3. Recognize your limitations. Everyone has limitations. At 10, 30, or 60, you can do whatever you seek out to do. BUT there are certain things that you may not achieve because of physical, mental, or emotional reasons. That is OK! The important thing is to not do anything that is going to hurt

you. Trying to *"do what everyone is doing"* was foolish when you were a kid. It is foolish now. If you need a reminder, go back and read my *"Everyone is trimming their hair down there"* story.

Choose Your Age

Chronological age is just a number. Real age is a mindset.

Please don't lie about your age. Own it. Just make sure you act your age... your way.

> *"You can't help getting older,*
> *but you don't have to get old."*
> – George Burns

CHAPTER 7

SEASONS CHANGE. PEOPLE CHANGE.

At our age, our parents may require more of our attention – a little at first, then more as the years pass. While it is the circle of life, this change takes a growing amount of your time. It can also tap your physical, mental, and emotional energy. It can be a draining experience.

And Don't Forget The Kids

Women are the primary caregivers in most families. Children are a big part of that caregiving. When the time has come for those children to leave the nest, their parents are supposed to experience *"empty nest"* syndrome. Empty nesters experience this time in their lives in one of two ways...

1. *"Hot diggity, they're gone. Now we can focus on ourselves!"*

2. *"My baby! He can't live without me!"* Translation: I can't live without taking care of him.

Well, that has changed. The financial environment of the world has changed the culture. Many adult children continue to live with their parents well past high school and college. Under the premise of *"saving money"* these adult children may live with their parents with varying degrees of independence throughout their 20s.

Then there are the *"boomerang kids."* These adult children move out... and come back. Sometimes multiple times.

Excuse Me. I Didn't Order This Sandwich.

We are now the *"sandwich generation."* Sandwiched between kids and parents. Each wants our time and other resources. This can age our mindset, if we let it.

To survive being squished in the sandwich, self-care is critical to maintaining our health, sanity, and positive mindset. It isn't selfish. Self-care doesn't mean *"me first"*; it means *"me too."*

Friends Are Friends Forever... Not

Are you still friends with your best friend from kindergarten? Probably not. That doesn't mean the relationship wasn't important at the time. But for everything in life, there is a season. We are not the same person we were in kindergarten or even 10 years ago. The people in our lives may change as we do.

Other people change too, so don't take it personally if a friend moves away from you instead of you moving away from her.

Sometimes we are blessed to have lifetime friendships. My besties, Jennifer, Lynn, and Laurel, were my bridesmaids in 1985. Today, they are three of my greatest treasures. Even though we live in three states and don't see each other very often, there is a bond that withstands every season. If any of those ladies called me at 2 AM (like I did to Lynn and Laurel one time... but that is a different story), I would jump into my car and be there. I know they would do the same for me.

One Of The Good Things That Came Out Of COVID

COVID made us find new ways of doing things, including how to communicate when we couldn't be with people in person. I adopted that mindset and now meet regularly with each of my important friends online or on the phone. We spend more time together now than we have in years.

It is OK when the time has come to move on from friends and make new ones. That's normal. But don't let *"life got in the way"* be an excuse for not staying in touch with your dearest friends. Phone calls, video calls, and getting together at each other's houses are a few of the ways we can stay connected. Supporting each other is invaluable. Whether it is a new relationship or an old one, treasure it. Nurture it. Having friends is a gift that not everyone has.

The Time Comes

As we get older, more of our friends and family pass away. In addition to the emotions connected to the loss, for some people, it emphasizes their mortality and they can become sad, depressed, and even sour. It may be hard, but try not to be one of those people. Don't allow those emotions to steal the quality of your remaining months, years, or decades. When you pass away, would you want those left behind to be less happy than they could be? Of course not. Neither do your departed friends.

When you do think of those who have died, don't just acknowledge it. Celebrate their life. Whether they were with you for six months or six decades, they changed your life in some positive way. Thank them in your heart.

Be The Person YOU Want To Be

Human beings can be frustrating, selfish, and sometimes, just plain mean. But they can also be kind, generous, and supportive. As you look at your relationships, now or from the past, remember *"You are going to make a difference whether you want to or not."* (Ken McArthur's Manifesto.) People make a thumbprint on your life – sometimes, a footprint. In the end, the majority of the differences are positive.

Relationships can be hard sometimes. But humans are created as social beings. Don't turn away everyone who reaches out to you. Nurture the relationships you have. They have helped to make you the wonderful person that you are today.

"There is a natural ebb and flow of friendships. The special ones survive."
– Colette McBeth

CHAPTER 8

WHAT DO YOU WANT TO BE WHEN YOU GROW UP?

When we were young, we had aspirations to be ballerinas, TV stars, and astronauts. When we graduated from high school, we needed to decide what our future would look like. Today, we are at the crossroads again to decide what we want to be when we *"grow up."*

It isn't too late to renew previous desires from your past. You may not be a prima ballerina, but you can dance. Maybe you aren't ready to be a TV star, but you can be the star of your own podcast. Don't think you can be an astronaut? Read on.

What Do You Think?

As your children move out of the house (eventually) and you prepare for retirement, it is normal to question what is next. Am I still relevant? Can I still provide value?

The short answer is YES!

Too many people fall prey to the lie that if they aren't working inside or outside of the house as much, that they're no longer important. These thoughts can lead to isolation, depression, and depriving the community of your gifts.

Check This Out

Diana Nyad was the first person to swim from Cuba to Florida without a shark cage. She was 64.

Anna Mary Moses, better known as Grandma Moses, began painting professionally at 78. She produced 1,500 paintings before her death at 101.

Wally Funk became the oldest person to go to space at age 82. She is still the oldest female astronaut. (See, I told you that you could be an astronaut!)

At 57, Mary Serritella started pole dancing. At 71, Mary is now a nine-time World Champion.

What Are You Going To Do?

So you may not choose to be an astronaut, but there are a multitude of options that match your values, personality, and interests.

- Be a doting grandma. (Help your kids get a parenting break.)

- Start a second career. (Whether you are a Walmart greeter or a consultant from your first career, you are making a difference.)

- Volunteer for your favorite cause. (Don't have one? Be a classroom grandma, work for your favorite candidate in election years, love up pets at the SPCA, or help any non-profit.)

- Take up knitting. (Or pole dancing.)

At 79, my mom became my chauffeur when I could no longer drive. Not only was it a huge help to me, but we got to spend a lot more time together. It also gave my mom another reason to be relevant.

Just because your life is changing doesn't mean you still don't have gifts to share. Enrich yourself and others by being your new *"grown-up"* you.

"The relevant question is not simply
what shall we do tomorrow,
but rather what shall we do today
in order to get ready for tomorrow."
– Peter Drucker

CHAPTER 9

TILL DEATH DO US PART... SOMETIMES

Intimate relationships are a unique beast. If you do them right, you have made yourself vulnerable. So the good times are good and the bad times can be heart-crushing.

I love to see couples celebrating their 40th, 50th, or longer anniversaries. There is a story about a couple who was celebrating their 60th anniversary. That Sunday, the husband was asked to come to the front of the church to give his advice on how to create a lifelong marriage. He said, *"On our wedding day, my wife and I agreed that I would make all the big decisions and she would make the little ones. Do you know we have not had a single big decision in 60 years?"*

The Statistics

The American Psychological Association stated that in 2022 approximately 40-50% of first marriages end in divorce. Petrelli Law reported the divorce rate for second marriages in 2022 was even higher, with approximately 60-67% of second marriages ending in divorce. Well, that's depressing.

In addition to losing your partner, you will be experiencing other losses and huge changes.

Whether your partnership ended in divorce, death, or other separation, it hurts. The length and intensity of your relationship can determine the level of pain and life changes you will experience. There will be changes... financial, living arrangements, and daily routines. It can even come down to your friends picking which one of you they will continue to spend their time with.

Change is hard. The most important thing at this time is not to isolate yourself. Seek out the support of one or more *positive* people. Do not spend time with negative people. They are toxic... especially right now.

As hard as it may be to believe, the changes will slow down and some of the hurt will dissipate.

Next...

At some point, you may be ready for companionship. It may be spending significant amounts of time with a friend or family member. But maybe, you will be ready to develop a relationship with a potential new partner. Whether the new person in your life is for companionship, marriage, red-hot sex, or something in between, you are about to embark on a new adventure. Since you probably haven't dated for several years or decades, things will probably be different.

If your prospective partner is about your age, the *"rules"* will probably be about the same; you just need to *"get back on the horse."* If you choose to date someone younger or from a different culture, you can count on things being very different.

"So, let me get this straight, I'm putting myself out there after a long time AND the rules have changed? Great. I think I will go back home, lock the door, and eat some ice cream."

Good News

There are several good points about dating in your 50s. Most importantly, there is much less drama.

While the pool of available candidates is smaller than when you were younger, you are looking for different things now. You are no longer looking for a potential partner to have a baby with. (You aren't, right?)

That doesn't mean you can't date someone younger than you. It also means *you* can take the first step. Put on your big girl panties and say *"Hi."*

You don't need to hang out in bars to meet someone. Find like-minded people at church, by joining a gym, attending a class, or volunteering.

Don't be afraid of trying dating apps for any type of relationship – Ourtime, Zoosk, and Silver Singles are a few. This gives you an opportunity to *"build"* the type of partner you are looking for. Beliefs, values, hobbies, likes and dislikes, and even height and eye color are part of the dating app.

Fifty percent of people who have tried dating apps have had good experiences. But to avoid weirdos and serial killers, always meet in a public place and drive yourself as long as you feel you have to.

Your Parent's Rules Still Apply

The important thing to remember is not to be pushed. It is ok to want to take it as slow or as fast as you want. In the same way, you need to be aware of how slow or fast your new partner wants. If you are at different places, you both need to find a comfortable place for both of you. No matter what, do not feel pushed or push them. If it is a relationship that you both want, you will slow down to the slowest person's needs.

You're Doing What?

Should you choose to develop a new relationship, expect pushback from family or others. You are an adult. Hear them out, then do what you want or need. You do not have to explain yourself or cave into their opinions.

But just like unhealthy relationships when you were a teenager or young adult, people may try to dissuade you from continuing a relationship. This is where it gets hairy. Remember the sound of *"mo-om"* when you told your teenager they couldn't spend time with someone.

Maybe this time the roles are reversed with your adult children expressing concern. But *"daughter"* doesn't have the same impact. At least consider their concerns to see if they are legitimate. They could be. Are the protesters coming from a place of love? If not, be strong and stay the course. What you choose to do with your new relationship has to be up to you.

You Want Me To Do What!

Depending on your relationship, you may broach the topic of more intimacy, and even S-E-X. For most of us, this can be a tricky subject. Depending on your past sexual encounters, it could be a very tricky subject.

If you have been in a long-term monogamous relationship, sharing your body may be difficult.

Think hairy legs, gas, snoring, and talking while you are sitting on the toilet. Yeah, THAT difficult.

Menopause adds an additional component. Menopausal and postmenopausal women may experience a lack of interest. There may also be a physical aspect. As we get older, sexual activity might be uncomfortable. Remember my aforementioned 80-year-old vagina?

I can't remember where I read it (we haven't even talked about memory yet!) but there was a great analogy... *"My vagina looks like a cave in an Indiana Jones movie filled with cobwebs, bats, and skulls. I don't know how the skulls got in there."*

Dryness and lack of activity may be able to be offset by supplements and topicals. My new gynecologist, who looks 12, also recommended sex toys to get the cobwebs out. He even suggested some websites. That wasn't an uncomfortable conversation at all. Geez! By the way, adamandeve.com if you're curious.

Intimacy doesn't have to mean sex. Holding hands, kissing, cuddling, or sleeping next to someone may be your choice too. The most important thing is a caring, patient partner that doesn't pressure you into something you don't want to do. This is the same message you gave to your teenagers. The same rules apply to you.

No matter what you choose, companionship is important to all humans. Whether you find a new partner, or spend more time with friends or family members, don't choose to be alone. Your life will be fuller and longer.

"We want to be loved,
appreciated, and cared for.
To have someone we trust and laugh with.
These things don't change with age.
Why on earth would they?"
– Donna Dawson

CHAPTER 10

ALASKA, WALES, AND PARACHUTES

I think the first time I heard the words *"bucket list"* was at the release of the Jack Nicholson/Morgan Freeman movie, aptly named *"The Bucket List."* For those of you who are unfamiliar with the term, a bucket list is a list of things you want to do before you *"kick the bucket."* Things like driving a race car, visiting Italy, or jumping out of a perfectly good plane with a little piece of nylon material and a few cords as your only form of safety.

Make A List And Check It Off

Some people may think of these things as a pipedream, wish list, or *"what I want to do when I win the lottery."* But all of us have some kind of seemingly out-of-reach desire. Nothing is too unusual or improbable in your mind.

Whether on a piece of paper or in your mind, make a list. Have one thing or 100 on your list? No worries. It is YOUR list.

Lewis Carroll said, *"If you don't know where you are going, any road will get you there."* Yogi Berra said, *"If you don't know where you are going, you might wind up someplace else."* I say, *"Fill that bucket, then do it."*

My list is to be a mom (check!), go to Alaska (check!), write a book (doing it here!), and visit Wales (still on my list.) A parachute jump is the last on my list. I may need to become a little more senile before I'm able to check this one off. And if the jump doesn't end so well... at least my list will be complete.

To Share Or Not To Share

Don't let anyone discourage you from your list. It is *your* bucket, not theirs. With that in mind, share your list with someone close who will support you, like I did with you (one of the 10,612 of my closest friends who bought this book.)

I shared my desire to visit Alaska with my husband and daughter. We went in 2017. It was a dream come true for me. Even though her favorite part of the trip was finding the hot tub in every place we stayed, my daughter reveled in my passion. My then 8-year-old proudly told almost everyone we saw, *"This is my mommy's dream trip."* That made Alaska perfect.

It Still Might Happen

My grandma had been to Florida before, but one of my early bucket list items was to take her to Florida, just her and me. In my early twenties, I drove my 60-something-year-old grandma to Florida because I didn't think at her age she would ever get to go again. See chapter 5, *"The Stupid Things (young) People Say."*

We had a wonderful time, and my first bucket list item was checked off. By the way, grandma traveled to Florida two more times.

There may be some items on your bucket list that never get checked off. It could be because of money, health, or time. But don't give up. It might still happen. Ask 103-year old Rut Linnéa Ingegärd Larsson of Sweden. She earned the Guinness World Record when she parachuted in tandem with a parachute expert in 2022.

*"Jobs fill your pockets,
adventure fills your soul."
– Jaime Lyn Beatty*

CHAPTER 11

THE SHOW IS ALMOST OVER

Ben Franklin said there is *"nothing certain except death and taxes."* I can't speak to taxes, but I can almost guarantee that I am going to die some day. So are you. But before that day comes, let's live life on our own terms.

Clean It Out

After the challenge of cleaning out my 90-year-old grandma's house after her passing, my mom began clearing her house of the things she no longer needed or wanted. My mom cleaned out A LOT of things. It was a walk down memory lane, good and bad. She showed my brother and me many things from her childhood and ours. She gave us the opportunity to take some of those memories with us. I even took some of my gangly, metal-mouth, preteen pics. You can never have too many scary decorations for Halloween.

Remember this is YOUR stuff – your cleaning process. Not your kids, friends, or others. YOU choose what stays, is trashed, donated, or kept.

That includes whether you choose to begin to clear things out or not. Enjoy the memories and choices yourself. After you pass, let your kids throw away things that are too special for you to discard.

Remember this when you help your parents clean out their home. However, I don't recommend bringing home your gangly, metal-mouth, preteen pictures.

Have The Last Word

What do you want people to read about you when your death is announced? You can make this your choice. You may choose the traditional approach... name, age, when/where you died, those you left behind, your service location, and suggested organizations for people to donate to in your memory.

You can also create one that embraces your personality. I wrote my obituary in my early 50s. I have edited details over the years, but the essence remains the same. I chose a less traditional approach. Big surprise, huh?

When I do mention those left behind, I personalize it with messages like, *"My greatest Earthly gift, my daughter, Ada."* While I do reference my professional career, I emphasize my primary role in life as an Encourager. I give a few examples, then ask people to honor me by doing a random act of kindness. I end with a quote. It is not too far out there, but it is me. That is how I truly want to be remembered.

Some people (or their families) decide to honor the passing with a smile. Here is an example:

"Pat Stocks, 94, passed away peacefully at her home July 1, 2015.

This is an obituary for a great Woman, Mother, Grandmother and Great-Grandmother born on May 12, 1921 in Toronto, the daughter of the late Pop (Alexander C.) and Granny (Annie Nigh) Morris. She leaves behind a very dysfunctional family that she was very proud of.

She liked four letter words as much as she loved her rock garden and trust us she LOVED to weed that garden with us as her helpers, when child labour was legal or so we were told.

She was a master cook in the kitchen. She believed in overcooking everything until it chewed like rubber so you would never get sick because all germs would be nuked. If anyone would like a copy of her homemade gravy, we would suggest you don't...

Send them out with a smile.

I Hereby Bequeath...

One of the big surprises in my early life was how wonderfully nice people could become bitter vultures fighting over THINGS when a loved one dies.

A Will is a significant document everyone should have. It eliminates the pain, disappointment, and messiness of separating what is left behind. It is your stuff. You can burn your money and possessions in the fire pit if you want. You can donate your entire estate to the *"Foundation for the Protection of Red-Bellied, Pink-Eyed Tree Frogs"* if you want.

Communication From Beyond

As a 63-year-old mom to a 16-year-old daughter, chances are I am going to leave her before most of her peers' parents. It is important to me to leave letters and recordings behind for my daughter's big events I may not be there for – when she gets married, becomes a mom, hits menopause, and turns 100. I will also pepper in things that I know she will still need to be reminded of after I am gone: clean your room, wear clean underwear, and no you can't have ice cream for breakfast until you are 50. Ok, maybe I won't tell her to not eat ice cream for breakfast. Heck, I'm dead. I probably wouldn't have minded ice cream for breakfast. (Admit it. You are thinking about ice cream, aren't you?)

These letters and recordings aren't just for your kids. Remember your friends and tell them one last time how much you appreciate them. Life is short.

There are letters you shouldn't write as much as you want to. Don't send letters like:

Dear Jeff, I never liked you. And you have bad breath.

Only write what you would say to a person when you were alive. At least try really hard.

The Truth

But it is not about dying. It is about living life to your fullest. We have all heard that no one on their deathbed ever said, *"I wish I had worked a few more hours, closed one more sale..."*

There is a wonderful Tim McGraw song, *"Live Like You Were Dying."* It is powerful as it talks about doing everything you want to do in life now... before it is too late.

And he said
I went skydiving
I went Rocky Mountain climbing
I went 2.7 seconds on a bull named Fumanchu
And I loved deeper
And I spoke sweeter
And I gave forgiveness I'd been denying
And he said
Someday I hope you get the chance
To live like you were dying

That sounds like a bucket list to me.

None of us are promised another minute, day, week, or year. Neither are our loved ones. Don't wait to do the things you want to do *"when I have more money"* or *"when I retire."* Tell loved ones how much you love them. Tell them what you want to tell them now, not later.

Treasure every moment... and may you have decades of quality moments ahead of you.

*"Don't be dead now. That time will come.
Now is the time to be alive."*
– Sadhguru

CHAPTER 12

YOU'VE GOTTA BE YOU. I'VE GOTTA BE ME.

Aging is an adventure, at least if you do it right. Ok, so you are over 50. What are you going to do about it?

This is your time. Be what you want to be. Do what you want to do. Heck, you could even write a book. Live your best (mid)life!

"Beautiful young people are accidents of nature, but beautiful old(er) people are works of art."
– Eleanor Roosevelt

AUTHOR'S NOTES

Remember in the beginning of the book when I said women should support and encourage each other? I hope I have become one of those women in your life.

If you like this book, encourage more women to read it by writing a review on Amazon.

I just started my next book! It's 365 of my favorite funny and motivational quotes. Please help me out by sending your favorite quote to karen@whentheheck.com. I would love to include it.

Thank you for purchasing my first book. It really is about supporting each other.

"Nothing is impossible. The very word says, I'm possible."
– Audrey Hepburn

KAREN SAXE EPPLEY

I am proud to be 63. I worked hard to get this old... more than 60 years. It is great to be me. It took me most of my 60+ years to figure out who *"me"* is. I am happy to report that I like who I am.

Pablo Picasso said, *"Your goal in life is to find your gift. Your purpose in life is to give it away."* My purpose is to be an Encourager. Every day I strive to make at least one person smile. Anyone can do this by sharing a smile, (consensual) hug, or buying lunch for the person behind you in the fast-food line.

I live in south-central Pennsylvania with my husband, teenage daughter, and two cats, George and Pepper. Those are the names of the cats, not the husband and daughter.

It took me more than 10 years to write this book. But, I have already started to work on my next book, so expect its release when I am 75.

Thank you for investing your time and money in my book. I hope it made you smile while you learned a little bit too.

Aging Gracefully,
Karen

*"I can do all things through
Christ who gives me strength."
– Philippians 4:13*

CONTACT INFORMATION

Karen Saxe Eppley
Muse Media
2275 Dandridge Drive
York PA 17403

KarenSaxe.com
WhenTheHeck.com
karen@whentheheck.com